Trouble in Paris

I Talk You Talk Press

CONTENTS

CHAPTER ONE

Mariko Kato was excited. She was at Charles de Gaulle Airport in Paris. She was waiting for her suitcase.

Many other people were also waiting for their suitcases. Mariko had a small handbag and a larger black bag. She put the black bag down on the floor. There was a man next to her. He put his bag down on the floor too. She looked at him. He was tall, and had dark hair. He looked about thirty-five years old.

"The suitcases are taking a long time!" said Mariko, in English.

The man looked at her, then he looked away. He didn't say anything. He didn't smile at her.

Maybe he doesn't speak English, thought Mariko.

The suitcases started to come out. Mariko watched them.

Where is my suitcase? she thought. *I hope it comes out soon.*

While she was waiting, Mariko took her smartphone out of her handbag and switched it on. She had two phones. She couldn't use her Japanese phone in Europe, so she bought a cheap smartphone before she left Japan.

She opened her Facebook page and wrote:

----*I had a wonderful time in Rome. Now, I've just arrived in Paris! I'm waiting for my suitcase! I have six nights in Paris!!!!----*

After a few minutes, she saw her suitcase. The man next to her saw his suitcase too. They both moved forward to get their suitcases. Mariko took her suitcase off the belt. It was heavy.

I did too much shopping in Rome, she thought. *I can't buy too many things in Paris. My suitcase will be too heavy to take back to Japan! Now, how can I get into the centre of Paris?*

She walked back to her black bag, picked it up, and looked for the bus stop sign. The man was gone.

CHAPTER TWO

Mariko sat next to the window on the bus. After about 40 minutes, the bus arrived in the centre of Paris. From the window, Mariko saw cafes and boutiques.

There are so many cute shops! I want to go shopping! she thought. *I can buy one more pair of shoes…shoes are not so heavy…*

Mariko opened her guidebook. *OK, so I'll check in at the hotel, have something to eat in a café for lunch, go shopping, then visit the Orsay Museum in the evening. Tomorrow, I'll go to the Louvre, and the Eiffel Tower, and…*

---*We will soon be arriving at Opera.*---

Mariko looked up when she heard the announcement.

Opera! We are here! she thought.

Mariko picked up her bag and stood up. There were some other tourists on the bus. They stood up too. The bus stopped. Mariko and the other tourists pulled their suitcases out of the rack, and got off the bus. Opera was very busy. There were many people and many cars.

I need to find a taxi, she thought. She saw some taxis across the road. She crossed the road and walked up to a taxi.

The driver got out of the car and said, "Bonjour." He put Mariko's suitcase in the boot of the car.

"Bonjour!" said Mariko. "To the Opera Vino Hotel please."

The taxi drove through the backstreets. The streets were very narrow.

Wow! The buildings are really beautiful! thought Mariko.

Mariko saw a bakery and a small café. *I can buy bread in that bakery and have a coffee in that café,* she thought.

The taxi stopped outside a small hotel.

"Nine Euros please," said the taxi driver.

Mariko gave him nine Euros and a three Euro tip. The taxi driver took her suitcase out of the boot.

"Merci," she said. She took her suitcase and walked into the hotel.

"Bonjour," said the young woman at the reception desk.

"Bonjour. I have a reservation. My name is Mariko Kato," said Mariko.

"Just a moment please, Ms Kato," said the receptionist. She found Mariko's reservation. "Could you fill in this form please?"

Mariko filled in the form.

"Here is your key. Your room is on the fourth floor. The elevator is over there. Breakfast is served in the dining room over there, next to the elevator. Enjoy your stay."

"Thank you," said Mariko. She walked to the elevator and waited. She looked around. It was a small, old hotel, but it was clean, and looked comfortable.

On the fourth floor, Mariko got out of the elevator. There were only three rooms on the fourth floor, and there was a spiral staircase in front of her.

Mariko put the key into the lock and opened the door. She went into the room. It was small, but Mariko liked it. There was a single bed, an antique table and an old style chair. Near the window, there was an armchair. She put her bag on the floor and walked to the window. She opened the window and looked outside.

This is a nice view! she thought. She had a view of the quiet street.

She started to feel sleepy. *I'll have a rest, and then I'll go to that café for a coffee and some lunch,* she thought.

Mariko lay down on the bed and went to sleep. She woke up about two hours later.

She looked at the clock. *Three o' clock,* she thought. *I feel great. But I'm hungry. And I want a shower.*

She went to the window and looked down at the street.

That's strange, she thought. *I know that man. I've seen his face before.*

There was a man across the road. He was looking up at the hotel. When he saw Mariko at the window, he walked away very quickly.

Who is he? she thought. Then, she remembered. *The man in the airport! We were standing next to each other, waiting for our suitcases! But why is he here? Why is he outside my hotel?*

Mariko started to feel a little scared. She closed the window and sat on the bed.

Maybe he is staying in the same hotel? No, I don't think so. He was looking at the hotel. When he saw me, he walked away. Did he follow me from the airport to my hotel? But why would he follow me?

She looked out of the window again. The man wasn't there.

I should be careful, she thought. *We always have to be careful when we travel.*

CHAPTER THREE

I don't believe this! thought Mariko. She was in the shower, but there was no hot water. *My shower system is broken!*

She went to the phone next to the bed and called the reception.

"Hello, this is Mariko Kato in room four one one. I think my shower is broken."

"What is the problem?" asked the woman.

"There's no hot water," said Mariko.

"Oh, I'm very sorry," said the woman. "I'll send someone to look at it very soon."

"OK, thanks," said Mariko. She sat on the bed and waited. Fifteen minutes later, there was a knock on the door. She opened the door. It was the manager and a man.

"Good afternoon, Madame. We have come to check your shower," said the manager.

"I am the manager of the hotel, and this is the maintenance man. May we come in?"

"Sure, come in," said Mariko. They all walked into the bathroom.

The manager and the man were talking in French. Mariko couldn't understand them. Then, the man said, "Ah, I see the problem. I can fix this."

"How long will it take?" asked Mariko.

"About thirty minutes," said the manager.

"OK, but I'm very hungry. Can I go to the bakery and get some bread?"

"Of course, I will look after your room," said the manager. "I will stay here."

Mariko took her handbag with her phone, money, passport and camera, and got into the elevator.

She walked out of the hotel and down the street to the bakery.

She went into the bakery. "Bonjour!" she said.

The baker smiled. He said something in French, but Mariko didn't understand. There were many kinds of bread and many different sandwiches.

"A chicken sandwich please," she said.

"Here you are. That's seven Euros," said the baker.

Mariko paid. *That's expensive!* she thought. *I hope I have enough money to stay here for six days. Maybe I can't buy a new pair of shoes… but I need a new pair of shoes…*

She walked back to the hotel. It was late afternoon and it was sunny but cool.

I hope the weather stays like this for the next few days, she thought.

Just then, she saw a man. He was walking out of the hotel with a black bag.

It's that man! And he has my bag! she thought.

"Hey! You! Stop! Stop!" she shouted. The man turned around and looked at her. Then he started to run. Mariko chased him. The man was fast, but Mariko was a fast runner. When she was a high school student, she was in the running club. She was one of the best 400 metre runners in Saitama Prefecture.

"Stop!" she shouted. The man ran onto the main road. He ran through the crowds of people. "Stop that man! Stop that thief," she shouted. "He has my bag!"

How do I say that in French? she thought. *Maybe people here don't understand English!*

"Stop!" she shouted. "Police! Police!"

A young man started to run next to Mariko. "Are you OK?" he asked.

"No! That man has my bag!" she shouted.

Mariko and the young man ran together. The thief ran down a small side street. They followed him. Then he ran onto another main road. There were many cars, so the man couldn't cross the road. Mariko and the young man grabbed the man's arm and coat.

"Give me my bag!" shouted Mariko.

The young man hit the thief in the face and Mariko grabbed the bag. An older man in a suit came to help. They tried to hold onto the thief's jacket, but he ran away.

"Thank you so much!" said Mariko. There were many people watching now.

"What happened?" asked someone. "We have to call the police."

"A thief stole my bag," said Mariko. "I hope he didn't take anything. I'll check."

Mariko opened the bag and a black box fell out.

"What's this?" asked Mariko. She opened the black box. Inside there was a diamond necklace. "What's...what's this?" she asked again.

"Oh! Oh! Look!" shouted a woman in the crowd. "It's that diamond necklace! It was stolen from a museum in Rome last year! Remember? It was big news all over Europe!"

"Oh yes!" said a man. "It's the same necklace!"

Everyone looked at Mariko. The young man held her arm. "So, this is your bag?" he asked.

"Er, yes, but this necklace is not mine," she said. "I don't understand. I..."

"Call the police!" shouted someone. "We have found the necklace thief!"

"What?" said Mariko. "But..."

A police car arrived. Two policemen got out of the car and took Mariko away.

CHAPTER FOUR

"Are you going to tell us the truth?" asked the policeman in English. He was around 50 years old, and he was short and fat.

"I'm telling you the truth! I'm a tourist from Japan! I'm an office worker! I'm not a criminal! I didn't steal the necklace! I don't know anything!" said Mariko.

"But this is your bag. Why was the necklace in your bag?" asked the policeman.

"I don't know," said Mariko. "Maybe it isn't my bag."

"It isn't your bag? Ms Kato, you are changing your story. First, you say it is your bag. Now, you say it isn't your bag. Which story is true?"

Mariko wanted to cry, but she didn't. She tried to be strong. "I don't know anything about the necklace!" she shouted. "And I want a French-Japanese interpreter! I can't do this in English!"

"The interpreter will be here in a few minutes," he said. Mariko and the policeman looked at each other. They didn't say anything.

A few minutes later, a young policeman walked into the room. A young woman was with him.

"This is Simone. She is your interpreter," said the young policeman. He smiled at Mariko and walked out of the room. He seemed nicer than the short policeman.

Simone sat down next to Mariko. She started speaking in Japanese.

"I'm Simone. I'm your interpreter. Please tell me your story."

Mariko started to speak in Japanese.

"I arrived in Paris from Rome this afternoon. There was a man

9

standing next to me when I was waiting for my suitcase. I got my suitcase, and I took the bus into Paris city centre. Then, I took a taxi to my hotel. I checked in, and went to my room. I slept for a few hours. I woke up and looked out of the window. I saw a man outside the hotel. He was looking up at my room. It was the same man. The man from the airport. I thought it was strange. I felt a little scared.

"Then I tried to take a shower but my shower was broken. So the manager and a repairman came. I was hungry. They stayed in my room while I went to the bakery to buy a sandwich…"

"Wait a minute please," said Simone.

Simone repeated Mariko's story to the policeman in French.

Then, the policeman asked, "Where is the sandwich?"

"I dropped it when I was running! I saw the man walking out of my hotel. It was the same man from the airport. He had my bag! I forgot about the sandwich! I wanted my bag!"

"So, it was your bag?" asked the policeman.

"I think so. Well, I thought so. So, I chased him. Another man helped me. That's all! Please believe me!"

The young policeman came back into the room. He smiled at Simone. He said something in French to the other policeman.

"Stay here. I will be back soon," said the policeman. They walked out of the room.

This is a nightmare, thought Mariko. *I hope this is a dream. I hope I will wake up in my bed in the hotel.*

"Are you OK?" asked Simone.

"I'm very tired," said Mariko. "And hungry." She looked at Simone. "You speak Japanese very well," she said.

"I lived in Japan for a long time. My husband is Japanese," said Simone.

"Oh really?" said Mariko. "Where did you live?"

"In Tokyo," said Simone. "I taught French there for many years."

Just then the policemen came back into the room.

"We have checked the airport security cameras," said the young policeman. "We saw you standing next to a man when you were waiting for your suitcase. You and the man had the same kind of bag. He picked up your bag by mistake, and you picked up his bag."

"So you believe me now?" asked Mariko, looking at the short policeman. "I'm tired and hungry, and I want to go!"

"Yes," said the policeman. He didn't look happy. "We believe you now. But of course, we had to check very carefully. We will take you back to your hotel."

"Thank you. Do you think you can find the man? Can you find my bag? I want my bag back," said Mariko.

"I don't know if you can get your bag back," said the young policeman. "Probably not."

Mariko shook her head. "It doesn't matter. I just want to go."

"OK, please wait a few minutes. We will arrange a car to take you back to your hotel."

"This is good news!" said Simone. "But you must be careful."

Simone gave Mariko her business card. "If you have any more trouble in Paris, you can call or email me."

"Thank you so much," she said.

"I'm an interpreter, and the young policeman, Philippe, is my brother," said Simone.

"Oh I see! So do you interpret for the police often?" asked Mariko.

"Not so often. Most Japanese tourists have a good time in Paris. They don't have trouble like you."

Mariko laughed. "No, I'm sure they don't. I'm just unlucky!"

"Well, everything is fine now. Enjoy your stay in Paris," said Simone.

Philippe came back and took Mariko to the car park. It was dark outside. She looked at her watch. It was eight o' clock.

Another policeman was waiting in the car. Mariko got in and the car drove out of the police station car park. She looked out of the window at the streets of Paris. Between the buildings, she could see the Eiffel Tower.

The tower looks beautiful at night. So many lights! This has been a terrible start to my trip, but I will have a good sleep tonight, and then tomorrow I will go sightseeing, she thought.

When she arrived back at the hotel, the manager was waiting for her.

"Ms Kato, I'm so sorry. The maintenance man and I were in the bathroom. We didn't hear that man come into your room. He was very quiet. I'm very sorry he took your bag. We will give you a discount. Fifty percent off your hotel bill. How is that?"

"OK, thank you," said Mariko. She was very tired and didn't want to talk.

She went up to her room and had a shower. The shower was

working now. She was too tired to go out for something to eat, so she opened her suitcase and took out some snacks from Italy.

These are presents for my friends and family in Japan, but I can get them something else from Paris, she thought. She ate all the snacks, got into bed and fell asleep.

CHAPTER FIVE

While Mariko was asleep, three men were having a meeting in a luxury apartment in the Latin Quarter, near the Sorbonne.

"Where is Jacques? He said before six o' clock, yes?" said one of the men. His name was Michel. He was very tall, with blond hair and bright blue eyes. He was the leader of a gang of criminals. They were sitting in his apartment.

"Yeah, Michel, he did," answered Neil. "He said, 'My flight from Rome will arrive in the early afternoon. I will show the necklace to the buyer, and then bring it to the apartment.'"

"So where is he? Phone him, Neil," said Michel.

Neil tried to phone Jacques. "No answer. He's not answering his phone."

Michel covered his face with his hands and rubbed his eyes. He was starting to worry. "Do you think something bad has happened to Jacques?" asked Fergus. "Do you think he had an accident? Maybe the buyer took the necklace and killed him."

The three men looked at each other.

"We should go and look for him. He has an apartment on Boulevard Saint Germain. He might be in trouble," said Neil.

"Let's go," said Michel.

"We don't have a key to his apartment," said Fergus.

"We don't need a key," said Michel. "Neil can open any lock without a key."

Neil laughed. "Yes, I'm good at that."

"Fergus, you wait here. If Jacques comes here, call us," said

Michel.

"OK," said Fergus. He went to the kitchen and poured himself a glass of wine.

Neil and Michel went out of the apartment and walked through the dark streets. There were some people around, business people walking home, and some tourists. They walked past Café de Flore and Les Deux Magots. It was a cool night, but tourists were sitting outside, drinking wine and coffee.

Neil and Michel walked in silence down the boulevard. After a few minutes, they stopped outside an apartment building.

They looked up. "That's his apartment," said Neil. "The third floor. The lights are off."

The main door was closed.

Michel pressed the buzzer for Jacques' apartment and waited.

"He's not here," he said.

He pressed the buzzer for another apartment. A woman answered. "Yes?" she said.

"I'm sorry to trouble you Madame. We are here to fix the water pipes," said Michel.

"The water pipes?" asked the woman.

"Yes, we received an urgent call from Monsieur Jacques Dupont. He has a problem with his toilet. We tried to contact Monsieur Dupont, but he didn't answer. I think his buzzer is broken."

"OK," said the woman. The lock on the main door opened and Michel and Neil went inside.

They walked quietly up the stairs to Jacques' apartment.

"This is it," whispered Neil. He turned the door handle, but it was locked. "I'll do it," he said. He took some tools out of his bag. Michel stood on the stairs, watching for people.

After a few seconds, they heard the lock click open. Neil turned the door handle and opened the door.

Very quietly the men walked into the apartment. They had a torch, so they didn't switch the lights on.

"Neil!" whispered Michel. "Look here! In the kitchen!"

Neil walked into the kitchen. "It's the bag!" he whispered.

Michel picked up the bag. "Come on!" he said. Michel and Neil walked out of Jacques' apartment, closed the door quietly and hurried out onto the street.

CHAPTER SIX

When they arrived back at the apartment, Fergus was waiting in the living room.

"Well? Did you find him?" he asked.

"No, but we found the bag," said Neil.

"Open it," said Fergus.

Michel opened the bag.

"What?" he said.

He took out a woman's jacket, a guidebook in Japanese, a travel insurance card, and some cosmetics.

"What's this?" said Neil. He was holding a piece of paper. It was a map of Paris with a hotel name circled in red pen.

---*Opera Vino Hotel*---

He picked up the insurance card. "Mariko Kato," he read.

"This is a Japanese woman's bag. But why does Jacques have it?" asked Neil.

The men looked at each other. "Who is she?" asked Fergus.

"Does Jacques have a new girlfriend?" asked Michel.

"I don't know. But this is strange. Where is the necklace? And where is Jacques? And who is Mariko?" asked Neil.

"We will find out tomorrow. We'll go to the hotel. We'll get Mariko and bring her here. She will tell us everything," said Michel.

"I'm sure there are many Japanese tourists staying at the hotel," said Fergus. "How will we find her?"

Michel thought for a minute. Then, he picked up his iPad. He went onto Facebook and typed in 'Mariko Kato'. There were many people called Mariko Kato. A few minutes later, Michel said, "I found her! Look!"

He showed them a Facebook page of a woman called Mariko Kato. There were photos of her, and a status update. Michel used the translation function to translate from Japanese to English. He read the status update to Neil and Fergus.

----*I had a wonderful time in Rome. Now, I've just arrived in Paris! I'm waiting for my suitcase! I have six nights in Paris!!!!*----

"That's her!" said Neil. "We must find the necklace. And Jacques. Mariko knows something. We have her photograph, so we can find her at the hotel tomorrow. We'll talk to her."

"But if she gets frightened, she might call the police. Let's follow her. She will lead us to Jacques," said Fergus.

"Yeah, you're right," said Michel. "Let's just follow her tomorrow morning."

"Can she speak French?" asked Neil.

Michel looked at Mariko's Facebook page again. "No, on her Facebook page, she wrote ---*I only know Bonjour and Merci*---," he said.

"Good. She can't call the police if she is frightened," said Neil.

16

CHAPTER SEVEN

Mariko woke up. She looked at the clock. It was seven thirty.

She was really hungry. She got up, got dressed and went downstairs for breakfast. There were other guests in the dining room. She could hear many different languages. She went to the buffet table and put eggs, bacon and bread on her plate. Then she took a pot of yoghurt and an apple. She put them on an empty table and went back to the buffet table for some juice and coffee.

Coffee, she thought. *I need coffee.*

While she ate breakfast, she updated her status on Facebook.

She wrote: *---I'm having breakfast. Today I'm going to the Louvre and the Eiffel Tower.---*

Mariko thought about the day before.

Was that a dream yesterday? She took a business card out of her wallet.

---Simone Ikeda, Japanese-French Interpreter/Translator---

It wasn't a dream. I have the interpreter's business card. It really happened. Why did this happen to me? I'm just a tourist. I hope nothing bad happens to me today.

She put the business card back in her wallet. She finished eating her breakfast, had another cup of coffee and went back to her room to get ready.

My makeup was in my black bag, so I have no cosmetics. I can't do my makeup, she thought. *But it's OK. No one in Paris knows me. I'll buy some nice new French cosmetics before I take any photographs of myself.*

Mariko looked out of the window.

It looks a little cool today, she thought. *I'll need a hat and a jacket.*

She put on her hat and jacket, put her wallet in the pocket of her jacket, picked up her handbag, walked out of her room and locked her door. She got into the elevator, picked up a map from the hotel lobby, and walked out onto the street.

In the apartment in the Latin Quarter, Michel was on Facebook. He was looking at Mariko's page. Every few minutes, he refreshed the page.

"OK! Here it is!" he said. "Neil, Fergus, get ready. We are going sightseeing. We are going to the Louvre and the Eiffel Tower."

CHAPTER EIGHT

Mariko walked through the streets. It was a little windy and the leaves were falling from the trees.

Paris is beautiful in autumn, she thought. She looked up at the sky. *It's sunny. I hope it doesn't rain. I want to get lots of nice photos.*

Mariko arrived at the Louvre before it opened. There were only a few people waiting in line outside. She looked at her watch.

It opens in a few minutes, she thought.

She took some photographs of the museum, and looked at the Metro map. At 9:00am the doors opened, and she went in. At the entrance, the staff searched her handbag and put it through an x-ray machine. Then she went down to the ticket office, bought a ticket and took a floor map.

She looked at the map.

If I want to see everything, I'll be here all day! she thought. *I'll stay for the morning, have lunch, and then go to the Eiffel Tower.*

Mariko walked through the galleries. There were many other tourists. Mariko could hear many different languages. She stopped to look at a large painting. Behind her, a man stopped too.

Wow! thought Mariko. *He has wonderful bright blue eyes!*

She walked into another room. The man followed her. In the next room, there was another man. He was wearing a Manchester United shirt. He was looking at the pictures. He didn't look at Mariko.

Mariko looked at her watch. *I've been in here an hour, but I've only seen a few rooms!* she thought. She looked at the map.

I'd like to see the Mona Lisa. Where is the Mona Lisa? Ah, here it is. First floor. She started walking to the first floor.

On the way, Mariko stopped to go to the toilet. When she came out of the toilet, she noticed a man. He was facing the pictures, but his eyes were looking at the toilet door. When he saw Mariko, he looked away quickly.

It's that man with the bright blue eyes! Why was he looking at the toilet door? she thought.

She walked through the gallery towards the room with the Mona Lisa. She turned around. The man was not there.

I must relax, she thought. *I'm here to enjoy myself. But I must be careful too.*

She went into the room with the Mona Lisa. There were many people. They were holding up smartphones, cameras and tablets, trying to take photos.

Mariko waited until she could get to the front of the crowd and took a photograph.

What next, she thought. She walked out of the room and looked at the map.

When she was looking at the map, she felt something strange. She looked up, and saw the man in the Manchester United shirt. He was pointing at her. She looked to the left. She could see another man. It was the man with the bright blue eyes. He was looking at the other man.

The two men walked away.

Why was he pointing at me? Why are they following me? thought Mariko. She suddenly felt frightened. *There is something strange happening. I have to get out of here.*

She looked at the map again. *Where is the nearest exit…*

Mariko hurried through the museum. It was getting very busy now. There were many tourists. She reached the exit and turned around. She could see the man in the Manchester United shirt. He was a few metres behind her. The man with the blue eyes was behind him.

They are following me, she thought. *But who are they? I should call the police. But first, I have to get out.*

CHAPTER NINE

Mariko went up the escalator and walked out of the museum into the sun.

Can I call the police? I can't speak French. Will they understand English? I have to escape.

Mariko walked very quickly. She turned around. The men were still behind her. She crossed the road and went down into the Palais Royal Musee de Louvre Metro station.

I will be safe on the Metro, she thought. *There will be many people. The men won't do anything to me there.*

There was a woman buying a ticket at one of the ticket machines.

How do I use the machine? she thought. She said to the woman in front of her, "Excuse me, could you help me buy a ticket please?"

"Oui," she said. The woman helped her buy the ticket.

"Merci," said Mariko. The woman smiled and walked through the ticket gates. Mariko followed her to the platform.

Come on train! she thought. *Come before those men can buy tickets!*

But the train didn't come. The men walked onto the platform. They stood a few metres away from her.

What should I do? Should I ask someone to help? she thought.

Then, she heard the train. The train stopped and she got on. She stood next to a group of women. They were talking very loudly. The man with the bright blue eyes and the man wearing the football shirt got on the train and stood at the other end of the carriage.

Where am I going? she thought. *I should go to a place with many people. A place with many tourists. The Eiffel Tower! Yes! There will be many English speakers there, and many Japanese speakers too.* She looked at the Metro map. *I have to change at Charles de Gaulle-Etoile Station.*

The train arrived at the station and she hurried to the next train line. Many tourists were catching the train to the Eiffel Tower. She stood on the platform and turned around. The two men were not there.

They're not here! she thought. *They've gone! Maybe they didn't see me!*

The train came. She got on and found a corner seat.

What should I do? she thought. *They might know my hotel. They might come to find me tonight. I have to tell someone. Who can I tell?*

She thought for a few seconds. *Simone! Yes! I can email her. She can help me! She can tell the police for me. I will email her when I get off the train.*

Fergus was bored. He was standing near the Eiffel Tower, looking for Mariko.

I hope she comes soon, he thought. *It's nearly lunchtime. I'm hungry.*

His phone rang.

"Hello?"

"It's Neil. Go to Bir Hakeim Station. She saw us at the museum. I think she'll go to the police. Don't wait at the Eiffel Tower. Take the car and park near the station. Bring her back to the apartment. If she tries to scream, show her the gun. We'll see you at the apartment."

"The car is already parked near the station. I'll go there now," said Fergus. He hurried towards the station.

Mariko got off the train and walked out of Bir Hakeim Station. She stood at the side of the Metro steps and started to type an email in Japanese on her smartphone.

---Simone, This is Mariko. Some men were following me in the Louvre this morning. Then they followed me onto the Metro. I think I lost them, but….

Just then, a man grabbed her arm.

"Follow me. Don't scream or I will kill you. Get in the car," he said quietly in English.

Mariko looked at him. He was big. He had red hair and he had an angry face. She looked around. There were many tourists, but they didn't look at Mariko or the man.

"I'll kill you," he said again. She looked down and saw a gun in his hand. "Get in the car."

Mariko put her phone in her pocket, nodded and followed the

man to the car.

CHAPTER TEN

Mariko looked around the apartment. It was a luxury apartment. There were expensive paintings on the walls. There were black sofas and a large table in the middle of the room.

Mariko was sitting on one of the sofas. Three men were sitting opposite her on another sofa. They were the two men from the Louvre, and the red-haired man.

"So, where's Jacques?" asked the man with the blue eyes. Mariko thought he was the leader. His English was difficult for Mariko to understand.

"Jacques? Who is Jacques?" asked Mariko.

The man laughed. "I'm not a fool. Don't lie to me Mariko."

"How do you know my name?" she asked.

"Where is Jacques?" he asked again. "If you tell us, you can go. If you don't tell us, there will be trouble."

"I don't know Jacques and I don't know where he is," said Mariko. "I'm just a tourist from Japan."

"Are you his girlfriend? Are you protecting him?" asked the man in the football shirt. He sounded like a native speaker of English.

"What? I told you! I don't know him!" said Mariko.

The men looked at each other. The leader stood up and walked over to her. "Tell us everything you know."

I have to get out of here, thought Mariko. *These are dangerous people. What can I do?*

She had an idea. She looked up at the man.

"OK, I'll tell you about Jacques. But first, I want to go to the toilet," she said.

The men looked at each other.

"She'll call the police from the toilet," said the man with the red hair.

"Give us your phone," said the leader.

"Here," she said. She gave the man her Japanese phone.

"And your bag," he said. She gave him her bag.

He pointed to a door. "It's there. There are no windows, so you can't try to escape."

Mariko went into the toilet and locked the door. She took her smartphone out of her pocket and took Simone's business card out of her wallet. She sent an email.

---*Simone, call the police. Some men followed me. They have a gun. Now I'm at their apartment. I don't know the address. I will try to get them to the Eiffel Tower. Tell the police to go to the Eiffel Tower! Don't reply to me. They will hear my phone.----*

CHAPTER ELEVEN

Mariko went back into the room. The red-haired man was cleaning his gun. She felt very frightened. She sat down on the sofa.

"OK, I'll tell you everything. Then, please let me go. I planned to meet Jacques at the Eiffel Tower at one o'clock this afternoon. He is not my friend. I just met him in a café yesterday afternoon. He said, 'Let's go sightseeing tomorrow afternoon. I'll meet you at the Eiffel Tower. I will show you something very special. Something from Italy.'

"I'm not interested in anything from Italy. I've already been to Italy. I'm interested in the Eiffel Tower. And Jacques is handsome. I was looking forward to going sightseeing with him."

The men started to talk in French.

"Neil, do you think she is telling the truth?" asked Michel.

Neil was the man in the football shirt. He looked at Mariko. "I think so. Jacques always finds women in cafes. The special thing from Italy is the necklace. I'm sure of it."

He doesn't speak French very well, thought Mariko. *Maybe his native language is English. His English is good.*

The red-haired man stood up and started walking up and down the room. "So he took the necklace! I'll kill him! I'll kill him!"

"Relax Fergus! We don't know yet. Let's go to the Eiffel Tower. He will be there waiting for her," said Neil.

"If she is telling the truth," said Michel, looking carefully at Mariko.

Fergus looked at her and said, "If you are lying, we will kill you."

Mariko looked at him. She thought he was the most dangerous. He didn't say much, but he always looked and sounded angry.

I hope Simone got my message, she thought.

CHAPTER TWELVE

The men and Mariko got in the car. Neil was driving. He locked all the doors. Mariko looked out of the window as the car drove through the streets. The streets were busy and there were many people around.

No one was looking at the car. She looked out for police cars, but she didn't see any. Between the buildings, she could see the Eiffel Tower getting closer.

"Which part of the Eiffel Tower did you plan to meet Jacques?" asked Neil.

"Near the ticket office," said Mariko.

The men started talking in French. Then, Michel said, "Wait for him near the ticket office. We will watch you. If you try to escape alone, or with Jacques, we will kill you. You'll never see your family again."

Mariko thought about her family in Saitama. She thought about her mother and father. Her father gave her some money to spend on her trip. He drove her to Narita Airport. He didn't want her to travel alone, but she told him, 'I'll be fine. You worry too much'.

If my family could see me now, she thought. *They would be very worried.*

The Eiffel Tower was now very close. The car slowed down and stopped. They got out.

Mariko looked up at the tower and all the people around.

"Well, go on!" said Neil. "Go!"

Mariko walked slowly towards the tower.

Where are the police? she thought.

She turned around. There were many people all around her. She could see Neil's head in the crowd.

What should I do if the police aren't here? Should I tell a security guard? This is a very public place. There are many people around. I don't think they will try to kill me here.

Mariko passed a group of Japanese tourists. They were taking photos of the tower and laughing. They smiled at Mariko when she walked past.

Should I ask them for help? No, the gang might do something bad to them, she thought.

Mariko was nearly at the tower entrance. She couldn't see any police.

Simone didn't get my message, she thought. *What am I going to do?*

She turned around. She could see Neil. Now he had a cap on, and he had a camera. He looked like a tourist.

On the other side, she could see Fergus. He was standing behind a group of people.

Then, everything happened very fast. Suddenly, two different men grabbed Mariko. She had no time to scream. They pulled her away. She tried to escape but she couldn't. The men were too strong. Then she heard lots of shouting and screaming. She tried to turn around, but she couldn't.

While this was happening, Michel was waiting in the car near the Eiffel Tower. There was a small black car parked in front of him, and another one behind him.

He saw two men pulling a young woman towards the road. She was screaming.

"What?" he said. "That looks like Mariko! Who are those men?"

Michel had no time to think. Suddenly, three men got out of the black car in front. They were pointing their guns at him.

The men pushed Mariko into the car behind Michel's car.

"Who are you? What are you doing?" shouted Mariko.

But the men didn't answer. They drove very quickly away from the Eiffel Tower.

"I'll call the police!" she said. She tried to get out of the car, but the door was locked.

One of the men turned around and smiled at her.

"We are the police," he said.

The car drove into the police station car park. Mariko relaxed and smiled. Then, she started to cry. She saw Simone run out of the police station. Simone pulled Mariko out of the car and hugged her.

CHAPTER THIRTEEN

Mariko and Simone were sitting in an office in the police station. Philippe brought them some coffee.

"Thank you," said Mariko.

"You were lucky, Mariko. And very brave. Those men are dangerous. They are part of an international gang. They steal jewellery and other expensive things," said Philippe.

"Please tell me the full story," said Mariko.

Philippe sat down opposite Mariko and Simone.

"Well, the man at the airport was Jacques Dupont. He was a member of the gang. The other gang members, Michel, Neil and Fergus, were waiting for him to bring the necklace to Paris from Rome. They planned to sell the necklace. But Jacques wanted to be very rich. He wanted to sell the necklace, keep the money for himself, and then run away. He planned to leave Europe."

"Did you catch him?" asked Mariko.

"Yes, we caught him today. He was at the train station. He was trying to escape. He told us everything," said the policeman.

"So, when you and Jacques picked up the wrong bags in the airport, Jacques got a bad surprise. When he got to his apartment, he opened your bag. There was no necklace. He knew you had the necklace. He found your hotel address in your bag. He came to your hotel and took the bag with the necklace. You chased him, and the necklace fell out of the bag. We brought you to the police station. We thought you were a gang member, or that you stole the necklace."

"Yes, you did," said Mariko. "But I'm not a bad person!"

"Yes, we know that now. We are sorry, but we have to be very careful. We have to check everything," said Philippe. "So then, when we brought you to the police station, Jacques ran away. He stayed at a friend's house last night, and then today, he tried to leave Paris. The other gang members were worried. They wanted the necklace. So, they went to Jacques' apartment. They found your bag, so they found your hotel address. The next day, they followed you to the Louvre, and one of the men waited for you at the Eiffel Tower."

"But how did the men know my schedule?" asked Mariko.

Simone and Philippe looked at each other.

"You told them," said Simone.

"I told them? No I didn't!" said Mariko.

"Yes, you did. You wrote it on Facebook. Your Facebook page is set to 'Public' so anyone can see it. They were watching your Facebook page."

Mariko was shocked. "I don't believe it!" she said.

"It's true," said Philippe. "You must be very careful on Facebook."

"You should change your privacy settings to 'Private'," said Simone.

Mariko nodded. "I will!"

"So, Michel and Neil followed you to the Louvre. But you saw them. And you saw them on the Metro. They told Fergus to take you to the apartment. When you arrived at the train station, he showed you his gun, and took you to the apartment. The men thought you were Jacques' new girlfriend. They wanted information about Jacques."

"Then I emailed Simone, and told the men I planned to meet Jacques at the Eiffel Tower," said Mariko.

"Yes, and I saw your email and called my brother Philippe," said Simone.

"You were very brave," said Philippe.

"And lucky," said Simone.

"Did you catch all the men?" asked Mariko.

"Yes, we did. Thanks to you, we caught them all," said Philippe. "You helped us catch an international gang! You should be a policewoman!"

Mariko smiled and drank her coffee.

"How are you feeling?" asked Simone.

"Very tired," said Mariko. "I want to go back to Japan. This has been a terrible trip!"

"I'm worried. I think you have a bad image of France now," said Simone. "Most people enjoy their time in Paris, but you had a bad time."

"I know," said Mariko. "I was unlucky. Jacques and I picked up the wrong bags at the airport. After that, all these bad things happened."

Simone and Philippe started talking in French. Then, Simone looked at Mariko.

"Mariko, how many more days do you have in Paris?" she asked.

"Five more days," said Mariko. "It is difficult to believe I have only been here for one night!"

"Our parents have a nice farmhouse in the countryside near Paris," said Simone. "Would you like to stay there for a few days? My husband and I, and our children will come with you for the weekend. You can relax, and enjoy France."

Mariko smiled. "Thank you, that would be very nice, but I don't want to be any trouble…"

"Oh, it's no trouble. No trouble at all. The farmhouse is very big. My family enjoy having guests."

"OK, thank you," said Mariko. "I'd like that very much."

"OK," said Simone. "Let's go to your hotel and get your bags. I will call my husband. He can pick us up from your hotel."

CHAPTER FOURTEEN

When Mariko woke up the next morning, the sun was shining into the room and the birds were singing.

Where am I? she thought. She looked around the room. The bed was very wide and very high. The bed covers were blue with white flowers.

She got out of bed, walked to the window and looked out. There were green fields outside and she could see lots of trees. The sky was blue. She opened the window, and a light breeze came into the room.

She remembered. *I'm at Simone's parents' house,* she thought.

She could smell coffee. There was a dressing gown on a chair in the room. She put it on and went down the stairs and walked into the kitchen.

Simone and her mother were sitting at the table. They both smiled when they saw her.

"Good morning!" said Simone's mother. "Did you sleep well?"

"Yes, I did, thank you," said Mariko.

"Sit down, and have some breakfast."

Mariko sat down. There were many kinds of cheese, some ham, and different kinds of bread on the table. There were some small dishes of jam and bottles of juice and milk too.

"Help yourself," said Simone.

A man and two children came into the house from the garden.

"This is my husband, Hideo, and my children, Kai and Emi," said Simone.

"Pleased to meet you," said Mariko.

The children were about eight years old. They asked her many questions in Japanese.

"Where are you from? How old are you? Do you have any manga?"

Mariko started to relax. She enjoyed talking with Simone's family. After breakfast, Simone said, "We are going into the village today. There is a nice market. They sell fresh vegetables and wonderful fruit. Would you like to come? We could have lunch in the village too."

"Yes, I'd love to, thank you," said Mariko.

"Good. While you are here, you can enjoy the slow life," said Simone. "Forget about the trouble in Paris. Tomorrow, we can go to the local winery. It is very interesting and we can taste the wine. And the day after, we'll drive through the countryside."

"It sounds great," said Mariko. "People say we have many surprises when we travel. I've had some bad surprises, but from now, I'm going to have a wonderful time!"

THANK YOU

Thank you for reading Trouble in Paris. (Word count: 8,079) We hope you enjoyed it. The next book in the City Thriller series is Danger in Seattle.

There are quizzes about this book on our free study site I Talk You Talk Press EXTRA. http://italk-youtalk.com

If you would like to read more graded readers, please visit our website http://www.italkyoutalk.com

Other Level 2 graded readers include
Adventure in Rome
Andre's Dream
A Passion for Music
Christmas Tales
Danger in Seattle
Don't Come Back
Finders Keepers...
Marcy's Bakery
Men's Konkatsu Tales
Salaryman Secrets!
Stories for Halloween
The Perfect Wedding
The House in the Forest
The School on Bolt Street

Train Travel
Women's Konkatsu Tales

ABOUT THE AUTHOR

I Talk You Talk Press is a Japan-based publisher of language textbooks, graded readers and language learning/teaching resources.

Our team is made up of highly experienced language teachers and translators, who have all studied at least one additional language to an advanced level.

This experience enables us to design our materials from the perspective of both the teacher and the learner. We consult with both teachers and language learners when designing our textbooks and graded readers, and test our materials extensively in the classroom before publication.

We are a fast-growing press, and currently publish graded readers for learners of English. We publish new graded readers monthly.